Essential Question

How can others inspire us?

In the Running

by Frederica Brown

illustrated by Carlos Aon

CHAPTER 1

In His Own World

"Marvin, you've been playing on your computer for long enough," said Marvin's mom. "Turn it off and come out. You need some fresh air and sunshine!"

Marvin sighed as he did as his mother told him. He emerged from the family room, blinking a little at the brightness of the world outside.

His mom handed him a cold drink and a sandwich. "Have a snack," she said. "Then why don't you come and give me some help in the yard?"

Marvin looked unenthusiastic. "Mom, I hate mowing lawns," he said. "Do I have to?"

"I'll do the lawn," said Mom, "but you can sweep the driveway and rake the lawn. Come on, if you've finished your sandwich, we'll get started."

Marvin swept slowly. It was an oven outside in the sun, and he wished he were inside the cool, cave-like family room. After about an hour, Marvin finished. His mom was still mowing the lawn, so he went inside and turned on his computer.

Ten minutes later, Marvin was lost in an enthralling game of Galaxy. He played online with a lot of other players. Most of them were kids like him, who spent most of their free time in the virtual world. They shared a friendly rivalry as to who gained the most points in a game, and they chatted online about music and books and games they liked.

Marvin played until he heard his mom calling him.

"What does she want now?" he wondered.

He went out to the kitchen, where his mom was serving up dinner.

"There you are," she said, "I've been calling you for ten minutes!"

"Thanks, Mom," Marvin mumbled as he took his plate and sat down at the table.

"I wish you had more friends," said his mother, sitting down, too. "You spend too much time on that computer. Why don't you play a sport instead?"

Marvin said nothing as he ate. When he had finished, he said, "I don't like any sports, and I'm not good at them, but I am good at computer games. It is what I like to do."

The next day at school, Marvin dragged himself through the day. He liked math and he liked art, but that still left a whole lot of other subjects that he didn't like.

When at last he got home, he logged onto his computer with a sigh of relief. Life was way more interesting in the Nebula Galaxy. Online, he could do anything—he was adventurous and courageous.

He heard a commotion outside and looked out the window to see a moving van pulling up outside the house next door.

CHAPTER 2

The New Kid

"Someone must be moving in next door," Marvin said to himself. Sure enough, he saw a family carrying boxes from the truck to the house. There was a boy who looked about his own age. He was wearing shorts and running shoes. "I bet he's totally into sports," thought Marvin. "He'll think I'm weird because I'm not into sports. I don't think we'll get along."

Then he realized the boy had prosthetic legs. That didn't seem to be stopping him, though, because he was carrying boxes back and forth like the rest of his family. Marvin went back to his game.

The next day at school, Marvin saw the new kid. Marvin thought about saying hello, but he didn't, feeling shy. The new boy came over to him instead.

"Hi, I'm Ben," he said. "We moved in next to you yesterday."

"Yeah, I saw you," said Marvin. "It looked like hard work!"

"Not too bad," said Ben. "Besides, I thought of it as weight training."

"I'm not really into sports," said Marvin.

"What do you like then?" asked Ben.

"Computer games," said Marvin.

"Galaxy is my favorite," said Ben. "But we don't have a computer, so I don't get to play much."

"You can come and play on my computer sometimes if you like," said Marvin, surprising himself.

"That would be cool," said Ben. "After school today?"

"Okay," said Marvin.

Marvin's mom was pleased that Marvin was having a friend over, and she fixed them snacks and drinks that they gobbled up before heading into Marvin's room to play games.

Ben turned out to be quite a good player, though he was a bit rusty. But Marvin, being a great player, beat his score easily.

"I'd better go," said Ben after they'd played for an hour. "I have chores to do, and I want to go for a run, too."

"Do you run?" asked Marvin in surprise. "I mean, I thought with your legs…" It was the first time Marvin had mentioned Ben's disability, and he suddenly felt awkward.

"Believe it or not, I'm training for a half marathon," said Ben, grinning. "Thirteen miles. And my legs work quite well. In fact, a study has proved that runners with prosthetic legs have an unfair advantage!"

"Wow," said Marvin. "Maybe you're like a cyborg—you know, a person who has been rebuilt."

Ben laughed. "That's me, all right—Cyborg-Boy Ben," he said. "I loved running and other sports before my accident, and I decided that losing my legs wasn't going to stop me."

Marvin found out that Ben went for a run almost every day. He was always asking Marvin to join him, and Marvin always made excuses. But he was secretly impressed with Ben's courage and determination, and he was beginning to wonder if maybe he could do it, too. He decided to go for a run by himself, just to see how it felt.

He huffed and puffed around the block, which proved to him beyond doubt he was unfit. "But I'm not going to give up just yet," Marvin said to himself. "I'll surprise Ben."

One morning a couple of weeks later, after training nearly every day, he got up early and looked out his window. Ben was outside, doing his stretches before a run. Marvin laced up his running shoes and jogged out as Ben was just starting down the road.

"Hey, wait up!" called Marvin, causing Ben to turn around in surprise.

CHAPTER 3

The Race

Ben grinned. "Come on, catch up!" he called. "Great to see you out!"

"Yeah, but let's take it easy," said Marvin. "I'm not as fit as you!"

They ran without talking the rest of the way because Marvin was breathing hard with the effort of trying to keep up. When they got back, Ben suggested that Marvin enter the half marathon.

"No way. I can't run that far," said Marvin.

"There's still three months to train," said Ben. "You'll be able to do it by then."

"I'll think about it," said Marvin. "Are you coming over after school to play computer games?"

"You bet!" said Ben.

Marvin went running with Ben for another month before he agreed to run the half mar[illegible] By then he was feeling pretty fit, and there were still eight weeks to go before the big day.

The race was being held in a town about ten miles away. The course was a ribbon winding through the town. It wove up and down hills and over trails and roads.

Marvin's mom drove the boys to the race. They got to the start in plenty of time, wearing their numbers that had arrived in the mail the day before—Ben's was 394 and Marvin's was 395. They did their warm-ups and found a place in the crowd at the starting line. Then a man lowered the starting flag and they were off.

They started at a steady pace. The course was flat for the first three miles, so the going was not difficult, especially as they both felt fresh and full of energy. They were still running well as the course started to climb into the hills.

"How are you doing?" Marvin asked.

"Okay," said Ben. "My legs are rubbing a bit, but I'll be all right."

395
MARAT

It was on the last mile that trouble struck, as Ben got a terrible stitch in his side. He stopped and doubled over.

"Go on without me," he said. "You're nearly there, and we're near the leaders."

"I'm not going on without you," said Marvin. "We'll finish together—you can do it. Let's just walk for a few minutes." They walked on slowly, and a couple of runners went past them.

"This is so frustrating!" said Ben through gritted teeth. "It's extremely painful to breathe."

"Don't waste your energy in frustration," said Marvin. "Just try to take deeper breaths."

Another pair of runners went past them.

"Come on," said Ben. "Stitch or no stitch, we're going to run!"

Marvin felt better after the break, too, and he was ready to start running again. They started slowly and then picked up their pace a little. Finally, they turned a corner and saw the finish line ahead of them. There were people along the sidewalks cheering the runners along, and the boys saw their families among them.

They almost fell through the finish line as their names were announced over the loudspeaker—they'd done it!

They gulped water like thirsty camels after days in the desert before throwing themselves down on the grass.

"Thanks for your moral support, Marvin," said Ben. "I'm not sure I would have made it without you."

"Of course you would have," said Marvin. "But I wouldn't have made it without you. Funny, I actually enjoyed it."

"Me, too," said Ben. "But now, I'm really looking forward to sitting down and playing some relaxing computer games."

Summarize

Use details from the story to summarize *In the Running*. Your Theme chart may help you.

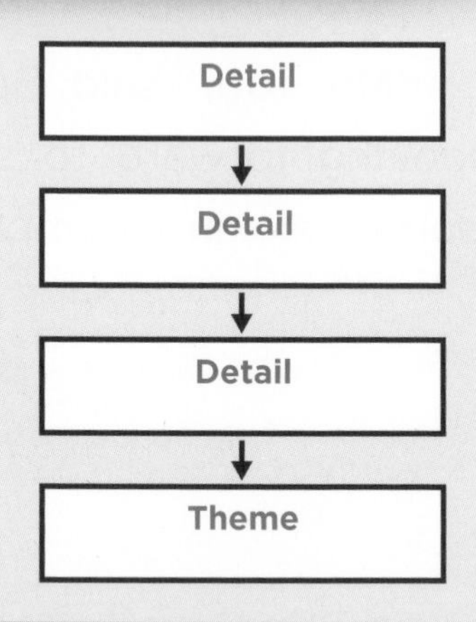

Text Evidence

1. What kind of fiction is *In the Running*? How do you know? **GENRE**

2. Why did Marvin start running? Look at page 9 for clues. **THEME**

3. What metaphor does the writer use to describe the race on page 11? **METAPHORS**

4. What was the message of the story? Use details from the text to support your answer. **WRITE ABOUT READING**

CCSS **Genre** Poetry

Compare Texts

Read how Suzy was inspired to start surfing.

Everybody's Surfing

Suzy was bored.
She was watching TV,
but there was nothing
very interesting to see,
when a show about surfing
came on TV.

Suzy was thrilled;
she was carried away
by the skill and the prowess
of the surfers that day.

She was inspired to try it
as soon as she could.
She went to the shops
and bought a wetsuit and board.

Suzy got to the beach.
She looked at the waves.
They looked bigger than
they did on TV—
it was hard to feel brave!

There were surfers out there
paddling out to the break.
She thought, Maybe I should
have tried first on a lake…

I will watch a bit,
dip my toes, take my time.
After all, surfing's cool,
there's no rush;
the day is mine.

At last she plucked up her courage
and went into the sea;
Everyone's surfing, how hard
can it be?

Splash! A wave came;
she was not nearly ready.
She was knocked off her board,
couldn't keep herself steady.

But she tried again, and then,
she was surfing. Indeed,
look at me! Look at me!
This is *better* than TV.

Make Connections

What inspired Suzy to take up surfing?
ESSENTIAL QUESTION

Who inspires you? How do they inspire you?
TEXT TO SELF

Focus on Literary Elements

Rhyme Poetry is language that is arranged into rhythms and patterns. Poetry often rhymes, too, but it doesn't have to. Poetry that doesn't rhyme is called free verse. A narrative poem tells a story. Narrative poems often rhyme, because a rhyme pattern can give a poem a sense of moving forward.

Read and Find The narrative poem *Everybody's Surfing* is written mostly in rhyme. Read the poem aloud to hear the rhymes clearly.

Your Turn

Choose a subject, such as a person, pet, or event, and write your own narrative poem. You can make it rhyme or use free verse if you prefer. If you choose to write in free verse, use repetition to help give your narrative poem rhythm. You can repeat words or just sounds. Repeating sounds is called *alliteration*.